Stories in the Sky

by Chanelle Peters

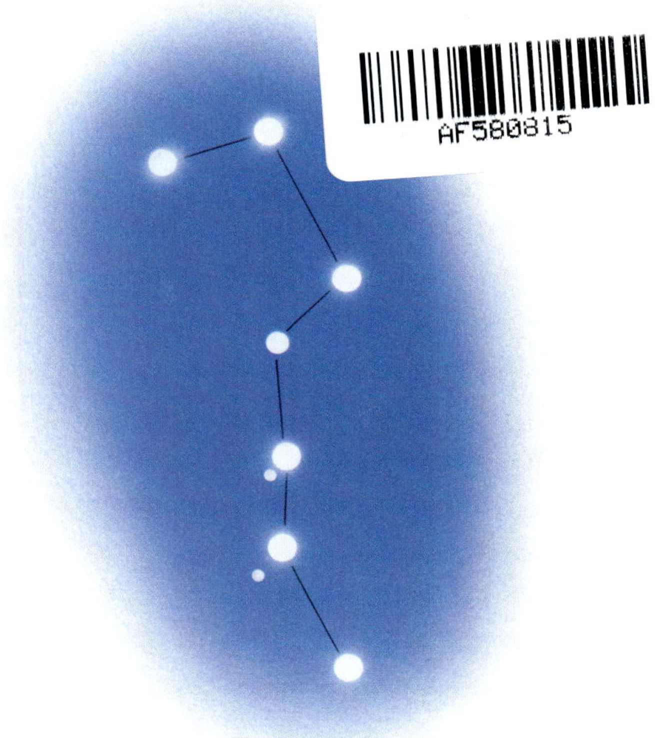

Scott Foresman
is an imprint of

Glenview, Illinois • Boston, Massachusetts • Mesa, Arizona
Shoreview, Minnesota • Upper Saddle River, New Jersey

Every effort has been made to secure permission and provide appropriate credit for photographic material. The publisher deeply regrets any omission and pledges to correct errors called to its attention in subsequent editions.

Unless otherwise acknowledged, all photographs are the property of Pearson.

Photo locations denoted as follows: Top (T), Center (C), Bottom (B), Left (L), Right (R), Background (Bkgd)

Opener: Brand X Pictures, (c)Dorling Kindersley; 1 (c)Dorling Kindersley; 3 (c)Dorling Kindersley; 4 (c)Dorling Kindersley; 5 Brand X Pictures; 6 (BL) (c)Dorling Kindersley, (CR) Getty Images; 7 (B)(c)Dorling Kindersley, (CR) Corbis; 9 (c)Dorling Kindersley; 10 (c)Dorling Kindersley; 11 (c)Dorling Kindersley; 12 (c)Dorling Kindersley; 13 (c)Dorling Kindersley; 14 (c)Dorling Kindersley; 15 (c)Dorling Kindersley

ISBN 13: 978-0-328-39436-4
ISBN 10: 0-328-39436-X

1 2 3 4 5 6 7 8 9 10 V0G1 17 16 15 14 13 12 11 10 09 08

When was the last time you looked up at the night sky? Have you ever wanted to **poke** your finger through the stars in the night sky? If so, you are like the ancient astronomers. They lived thousands of years ago. They spent their time gazing at the stars.

Ancient astronomers **imagined** that there were lines between some stars. To them the lines made shapes and patterns. These patterns became known as constellations. Each constellation has its own area of the sky. Many constellations were named after gods and heroes from Greek and Roman myths. People also liked to name constellations after animals.

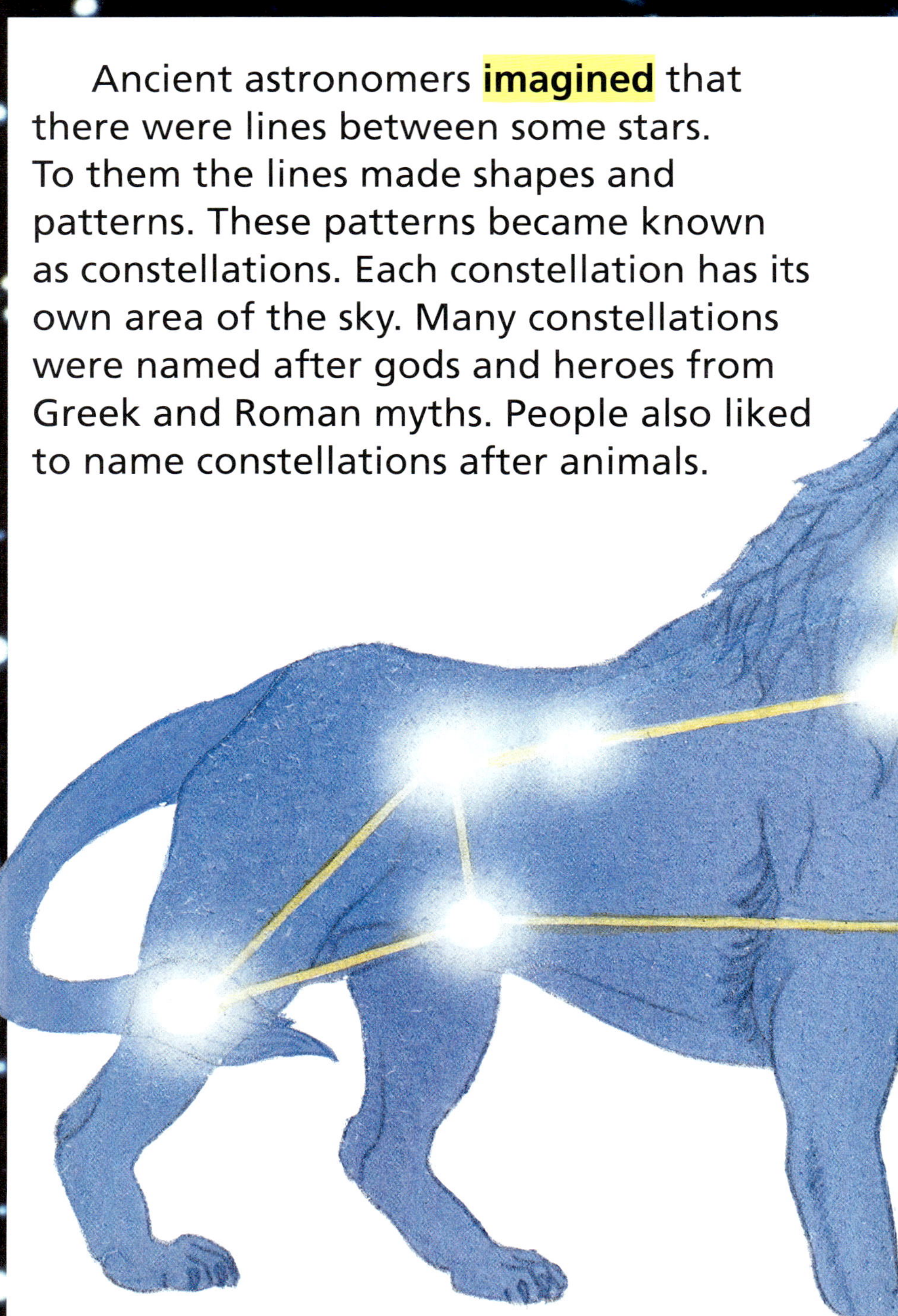

At different times of the year you can see different constellations in the sky. You may find it hard to see a shape in a constellation. That's because constellations only suggest things. They don't show actual people or animals. The stars in a constellation make up the outline of a shape or object. People have to fill in the outline using their imagination and what they have heard about the constellation.

The stars that make up the constellation Leo.

The astronomers of ancient Mesopotamia were the first to name constellations. Astronomers of ancient Egypt and Greece also named constellations. The first star charts had forty-eight constellations.

In 1928 astronomers from around the world met. They decided to organize the night stars. The astronomers placed the stars into separate constellations. They created eighty-eight constellations.

The eighty-eight constellations were given Latin names. Some you might know. One of the constellations is called Aries. Aries means "ram." A ram is a male sheep. Rams have horns. Horns are like **antlers**. Delphinus, another constellation, means "dolphin." Why do these names come from the Latin **language**? Because people who spoke Latin discovered and named many constellations.

Aries, which means "ram" (below left), and Delphinus, which means "dolphin" (below right)

Some constellations have very bright stars. These bright stars were important to ancient peoples. They gave them names.

Most of these stars have Greek or Arabic names. The constellation Gemini contains the stars Castor and Pollux. Those names are Greek. It also contains the stars Wasat, Mebsuta, and Alhena. Those names are Arabic.

You have already read about the names of the constellations. The constellations also have stories. These stories are taken from African, Chinese, Egyptian, Greek, Roman, and Native American mythology.

A myth is an old story that has been told orally for generations. Myths often explain how things in nature came to be. Other stories tell about amazing events involving gods and heroes.

An ancient Roman temple built to honor Castor and Pollux

The Greeks and Romans had many great astronomers. They gave names to many different stars and constellations. The word *astronomy* comes from Greek words meaning "star" and "law." The ancient Greeks and Romans used constellations to honor their gods, such as Juno and Zeus.

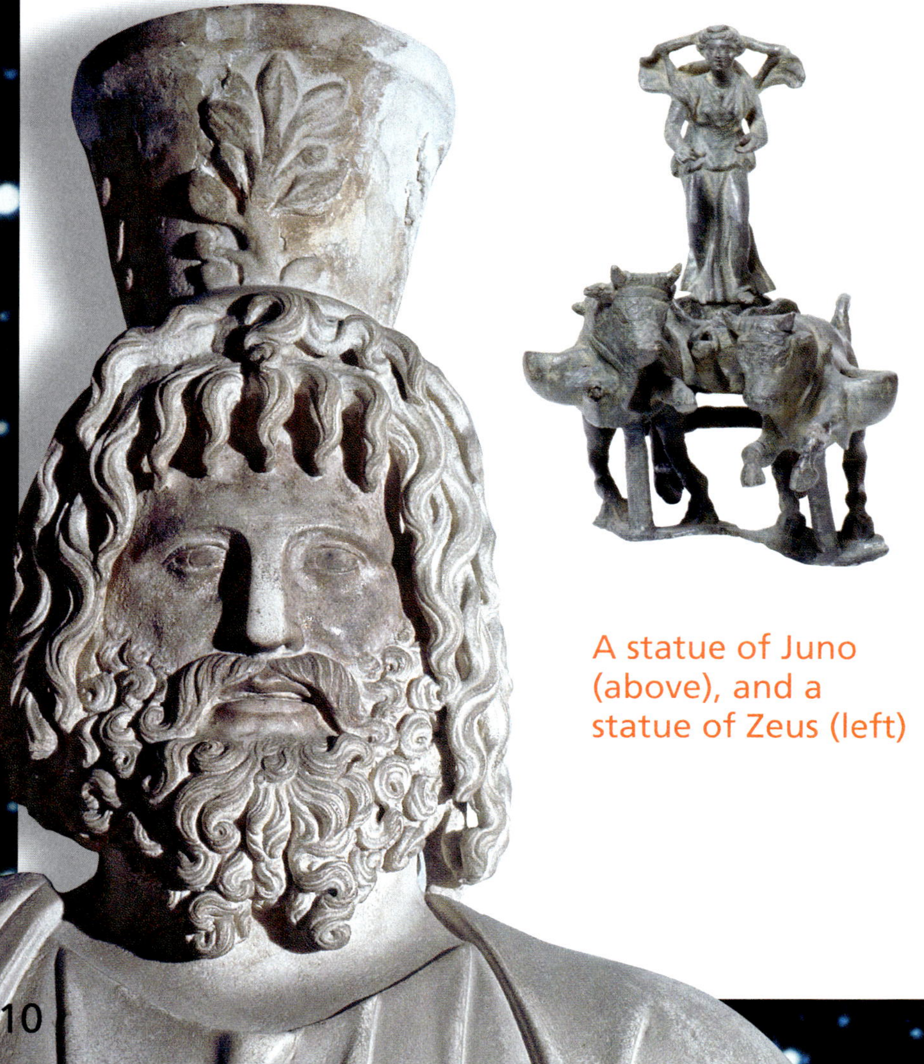

A statue of Juno (above), and a statue of Zeus (left)

The constellation Hercules

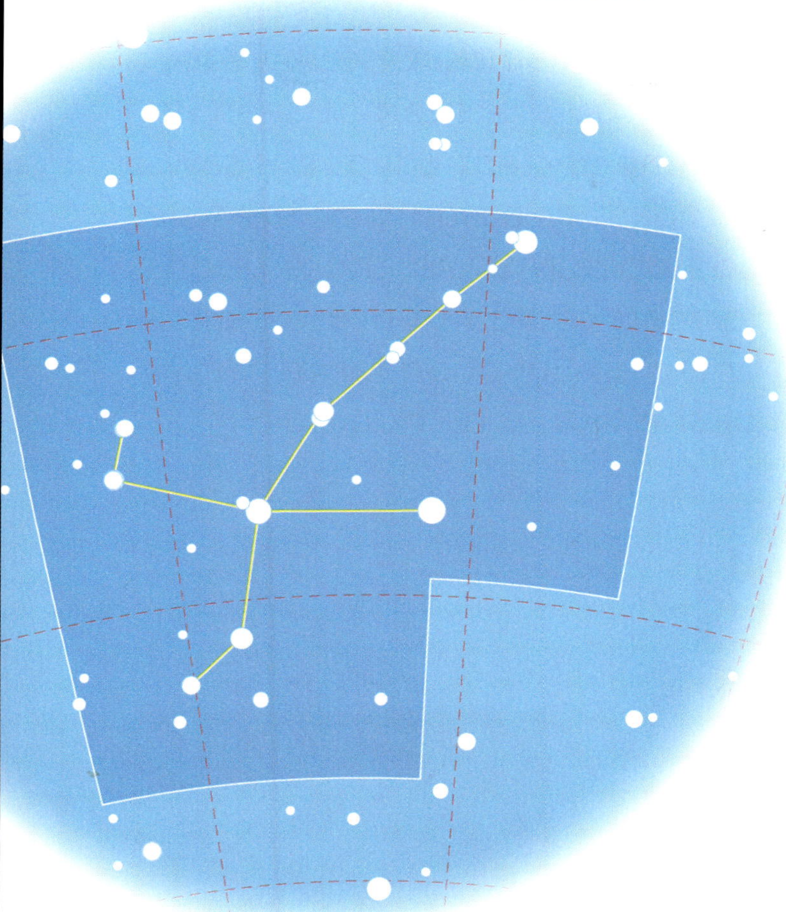

The Greeks and Romans spent many nights looking **overhead** at the night sky. Greek and Roman parents would point out constellations such as Hercules to their children. They would tell stories about this hero's great strength while looking at his constellation.

The ancient Egyptians also watched the stars. One of their most important stars was the star we call Sirius. Once a year just before sunrise, Sirius can be seen in Egypt. When the ancient Egyptians saw Sirius, they took it as a sign that the Nile River would flood. Without those floods, Egyptian farmers could not grow their crops. So when an Egyptian farmer saw Sirius, he or she would be hopeful.

An Egyptian stairwell, with a gauge for measuring Nile River floods (right), and a star clock (far right).

To people who lived in Africa, the cluster of stars called Pleiades was very important. One group of Africans, the Bantu people, believed Pleiades represented a plow. When the Bantu people saw Pleiades in the sky, it was time for them to begin plowing and planting crops.

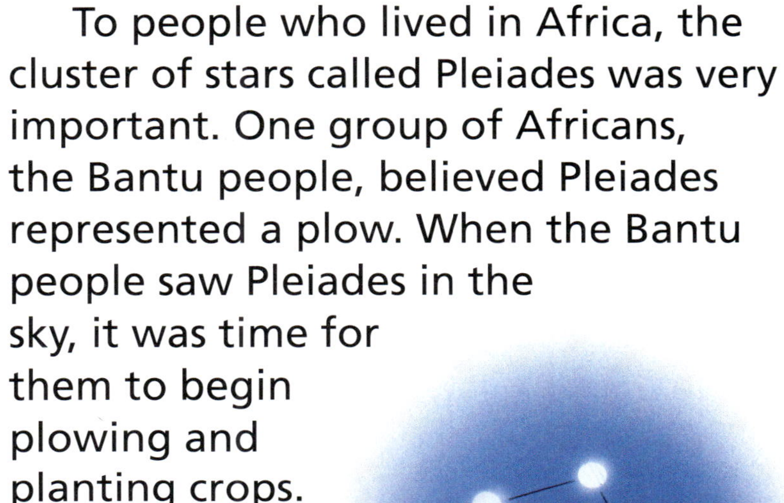

Native Americans tell a tale about the stars Sirius and Antares. They call them the Dog Stars. The **narrator** explains that when people die they travel through the sky. Then they have to pass the Dog Stars. If they feed only the first dog and not the second one, they will be stuck in the night sky forever.

The star Antares is part of the constellation Scorpius.

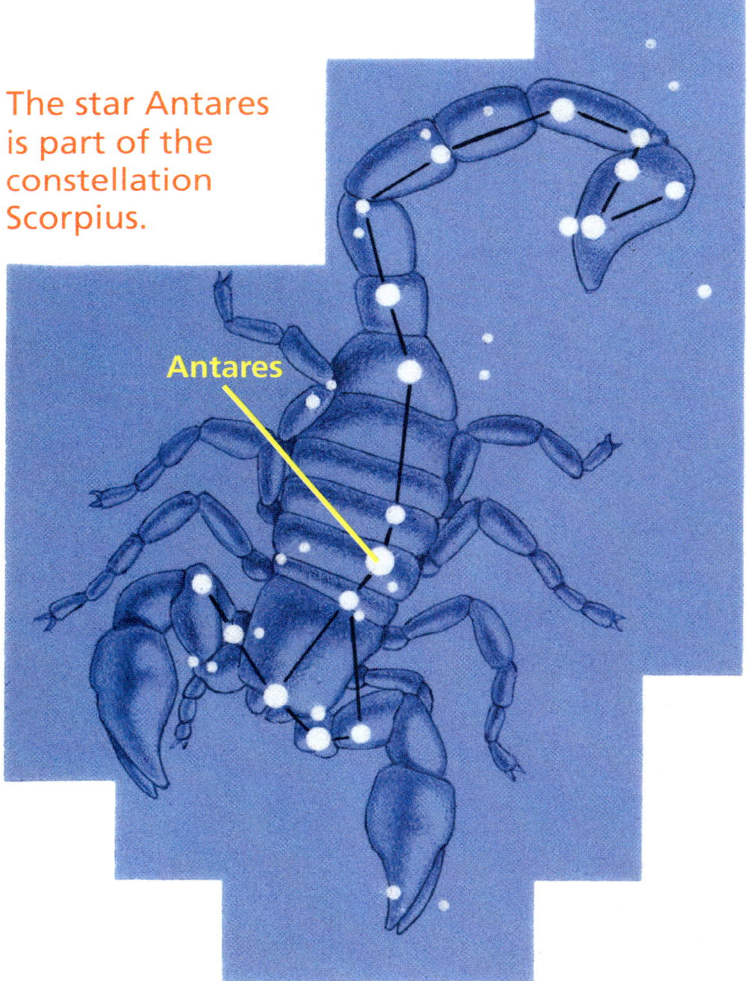

The star Sirius is part of the constellation Canis Major.

You've now learned plenty about the constellations. Think about what you've learned the next time you look at the night sky. You might be able to recognize the constellations talked about in this book!

Glossary

antlers *n.* bony growths on the heads of deer, elk, and moose that are shed each year. Antlers grow in pairs, and branch out. They are like horns.

imagined *v.* to have pictured something in your mind or formed an image or idea of it.

language *n.* human speech, spoken or written.

narrator *n.* a person who tells a story.

overhead *adv.* something you have to look up to see.

poke *v.* to push against with something pointed.